Contents

POST-IMPRESSIONISM

A clear insight into Artists and their Art

Pam Cutler

Barrington Stoke

First published 2004 in Great Britain by
Barrington Stoke Ltd, Sandeman House, Trunk's Close,
55 High Street, Edinburgh, EH1 1SR

www.barringtonstoke.co.uk

Front cover image: Starry Night (1889) by Vincent Van Gogh

ISBN 1-84299-177-9

Edited by Julia Rowlandson
Cover design by Helen Ferguson
Picture research by Kate MacPhee

Designed and typeset by GreenGate Publishing Services,
Tonbridge
Printed in Great Britain by The Bath Press

Barrington Stoke acknowledges support from the Scottish
Arts Council towards the publication of this title.

Scottish
Arts Council
LOTTERY FUNDED

Introduction

The name **Post-Impressionism** was first used by the English artist and critic, **Roger Fry**.

In 1910, Fry set up an exhibition in London of modern French art and called it **Manet and the Post-Impressionists**. Two years later, in 1912, he organised another big exhibition of Post-Impressionist work.

These exhibitions were made up of lots of artists but most of them had worked in the Impressionist way at one time. All of them had felt the Impressionist style was limited and had tried to go beyond it by developing their work in different ways.

Many people did not understand what these artists were trying to do so Fry wrote an article in the *catalogue* for the second of his Post-Impressionist exhibitions. In the article he explained and defended the work on show. He said that the reason why these artists were often misunderstood and not valued, was because people thought that the most important role of an artist was to paint what things looked like. Fry wrote that the Post-Impressionist artists did not simply want to copy life, but were trying to make paintings that would appeal to our imaginations and enrich our minds.

PART
ONE

catalogue – a book which lists artworks displayed in an exhibition and also has essays in it describing and explaining the work.

In order to understand more about what the Post-Impressionist artists achieved we need to discover the answers to the following five questions:

- Where did Post-Impressionism come from?

- What was Post-Impressionism?

- Who were the Post-Impressionists?

- What and who influenced Post-Impressionist artists to work in the way they did?

- What did the Post-Impressionists like to paint and what methods did they use?

Where did Post-Impressionism come from?

Post-Impressionism had its roots in Impressionism

Impressionism was at its strongest in the 1870s but by the last Impressionist Exhibition in 1886, its influence was fading and artists wanted to go beyond its aims.

However, it was Impressionism that had broken the control of the *art establishment* and paved the way for the direction art took right up to the early 20th century. Impressionism was an important movement because it threw out *traditional* ideas about art and set out a whole new set of problems for artists to tackle.

The changes the Impressionists brought about were:

1 They refused to stick to the old categories of high art laid down by the Salon (annual exhibition of the French Royal Academy of Painting in Paris) and the School of Fine Art in Paris, which said that history painting was the most important subject. Instead they chose to paint everyday subjects like Parisian street and café life, suburban leisure spots, picnics in the park, beach scenes, etc.

art establishment – those people who are recognised as being the authority on art. They included the Royal Academicians and the Salon jury who thought that art should only show idealised scenes of people and places.

traditional – a tried and tested way of doing things which is often handed down from one generation to another.

La Grenouillère (1869) by Pierre-Auguste Renoir.
Private Collection

This painting is a good example of Impressionist techniques and subject matter.

composition – the layout or formal design of a picture.

perspective – a way of constructing a picture from a particular viewpoint as though you were looking through a window into it.

transient – short-lived, passing opposite to lasting.

luminous – glowing with light.

complementary colours – colours which are opposite each other in the colour wheel, for example, blue and orange, purple and yellow, green and red.

2 They challenged *traditional* ideas of *composition* and *perspective*. They studied Japanese prints and used their odd viewpoints and designs in their own work.

3 They worked outside straight from nature or other subjects and tried to capture the *transient* effects of light by using swift dashes of paint.

4 They tried to achieve *luminous* colour effects by using *complementary colours* on canvases primed with white paint.

5 They decided not to submit work to the Salon and held their own exhibitions where the artists decided themselves what work to put on display. This meant that they were free to experiment and try out new ways of working, without fear of being rejected by the Salon jury.

The Impressionist's revolt against *traditional* rules and values had made it possible for Post-Impressionist artists to extend their subject matter, experiment with colour and try out new ways of structuring pictures.

What was Post-Impressionism?

The four major artists of Post-Impressionism were **Georges Seurat**, **Vincent Van Gogh**, **Paul Gauguin** and **Paul Cézanne**. They had all worked in an Impressionist style and had learnt a lot from it. They also valued the break with tradition that Impressionism had brought about but now wanted to develop their work further. They wanted to do something **different** from the **Impressionist** aims listed below:

1 The need to capture the moment in their paintings.

2 The importance of light above everything else.

3 The lack of focus on structure and form.

4 Leaving out symbolism and any references to anything outside the painting such as literature or mythology.

5 The desire to only work straight from nature or scenes from everyday life.

These Post-Impressionist artists all developed very personal styles, had different goals and chose different directions in which to take their work. Seurat focused on new scientific theories of colour; Cézanne on structure and form; Van Gogh on the psychology of form and colour; and Gauguin on the *symbolic* power of colour.

Who were the Post-Impressionists?

The artists who first made the break with Impressionism, and who are now seen as leading figures of the Post-Impressionist group, are:

Paul **Cézanne** (1839–1906)   Paul **Gauguin** (1848–1903)

Vincent **Van Gogh** (1853–1890)   Georges **Seurat** (1859–1891)

Other artists who are called **Post-Impressionists** worked within the areas first set up by these four main painters. Their individual interests and the artists they influenced are listed below.

Cézanne developed geometric structure in his paintings and influenced *Cubist* artists such as **Pablo Picasso**, **Georges Braque** and **Robert Delaunay**. In 1908 Georges Braque (1882–1963) painted **Viaduct at L'Estaque** which was one of Cézanne 's favourite places to paint. Cézanne's influence and the beginnings of *Cubism* can be seen in this painting.

Seurat's scientific theories of colour and line were shared by the painter **Paul Signac** and influenced artists like **Andre Derain** and **Maurice De Vlaminck** who were members of a group called the *Fauves*. **Henri Matisse**, who was the main artist in this group, also admired **Gauguin**'s use of flat areas of colour.

Van Gogh's use of colour and form to express his strong emotions and inner feelings were admired by **Maurice de Vlaminck** who claimed to worship Van Gogh more than his own father. Van Gogh also influenced Expressionist painters like **Ernst Kirchner** (1880–1938) and **Vasily Kandinsky** (1866–1944).

symbol / symbolic – a sign or object which stands in for, and refers to, a hidden or deeper meaning.

Fauves – comes from a French word meaning 'wild beasts'. In 1905, this name was given to a group of artists led by Henri Matisse who painted using a bold and shocking style with very bright colours.

Cubism – Cubist – a style of painting developed in 1908 by Georges Braque and Pablo Picasso. They made paintings which showed things from different angles at the same time and broke up their pictures into geometric shapes like cubes and triangles.

The Côte d'Azur (1889) by Paul Signac

Haags Gemeentemuseum, The Hague, Netherlands
© DACS 2004

Paul Signac produced this painting using the new Divisionist technique he had developed with Seurat.

symbol / symbolic – a sign or object which stands in for, and refers to, a hidden or deeper meaning.

applied arts – areas of design where artists' skills are used to produce things for a set purpose like posters and furniture.

A Family Evening (1895) by Edouard Vuillard

Private Collection
© ADAGP, Paris and DACS, London 2004

Gauguin's *symbolic* use of colour influenced a group of artists called the *Nabis* who included **Paul Serusier**, **Emile Bernard**, **Pierre Bonnard**, **Maurice Denis** and **Edouard Vuillard**. (See **The Family Evening**, 1895.) These artists believed that colour had the expressive power of music and could affect our imaginations and feelings directly.

These four major Post-Impressionist artists, Van Gogh, Gauguin, Seurat and Cézanne, had a huge influence on the direction of modern art. Their experiments and discoveries deepened artists' understanding of colour and form and led the way forward to the main movements of 20th century art.

Two other artists in this period, **Toulouse-Lautrec** (1864–1901) and **Raoul Dufy** (1877–1953) had a more lasting influence on the *applied arts*. Dufy's designs were very successful as textile prints and Toulouse-Lautrec got his name known as a brilliant poster designer.

What and who influenced Post-Impressionist artists to work in the way they did?

The rapidly changing world of 1880–1900

By the mid-1880s, Paris had become a huge city. It had even spread to the suburban (on the edge of the city) leisure spots painted by the Impressionist artists. France was becoming industrialised and factories were being built to produce goods faster. Many people had left the countryside and come to the cities for work.

Communication of news and information was faster. In 1860 there had been only four newspapers in Paris but by 1890 there were 70 daily newspapers. Transport was becoming faster and better. By 1900 railways, buses, trams and underground systems had replaced horse-drawn carriages in cities. Railways were built across the country. Progress was also being made in medicine, science and technology.

Post-Impressionism

There was a great interest in the peoples and cultures of foreign lands. In 1889, the Universal Exhibition was held in the *Palais des Colonies* (Palace of the Colonies) in Paris which had displays of people and their *artefacts* from around the world. The Anthropological Society of Paris was the first to classify the shapes and sizes of human types. It had collected together photographs of natives from the French colonies, and put them on show in ornate albums.

The Post-Impressionist artists were living through this time of great social change and responded in different ways to the events and ideas of their time.

artefact – a product of human art and workmanship such as a clay pot, poster, furniture, etc.

arbitrary – based on opinion not research.

luminous – glowing with light.

spiritual – involving the inner, unworldly side of human understanding.

The influence of new scientific ideas

Seurat believed that art and science could work together to produce a new and more systematic approach to painting. He thought the Impressionists' use of colour was too *arbitrary* and their brushwork was so individual that it took our attention away from the effect of the colours.

Seurat, **Signac** and **Pissarro** were the main artists who started a method of painting which was called *Divisionism*, *Pointillism* or *Neo-Impressionism*. Their method was based on current scientific research into colour and the way we see things. In **Le Bec du Hoc**, 1885, Seurat created a *luminous*, shimmering effect with lots of tiny dots of pure colour.

Le Bec du Hoc (1885) by Georges Seurat
National Gallery of Australia, Canberra

The search for meaning

Many people found the experience of living in large cities and in an industrialised society was one that made them feel lonely and sad. The rush for progress and material gain did not meet their *spiritual* needs. They searched for more meaningful or religious experiences and longed for a life that was more in harmony with the natural world.

To rediscover for themselves this hidden world of feeling, **Paul Gauguin**, **Emile Bernard**, **Paul Serusier** and others set up a colony of artists among the peasants of

vibrant – vivid, thrilling.

durable – lasting.

Brittany in western France. They invented a new style of painting which was based on folk art and the use of flat, areas of colour as in church stained glass windows. Gauguin's painting of **The Vision after the Sermon**, 1888 (see page 42) showed the silent devotion of peasant women experiencing a religious vision. This painting appealed to the *Symbolists*, a group of poets, writers and artists who wanted art and literature to be about deep, hidden meanings and mystery.

Self-Portrait (1889) by Vincent Van Gogh
Musée d'Orsay, Paris, France

The experience of the individual

The growth of industry and large populations in cities in the 1880s, forced people to accept and conform to a society which had little room for people as individuals.

Van Gogh's paintings are deeply personal and expressive. He was very upset by the values of industrial society and moved by the harsh conditions in which many poor people lived. He had a mystic faith in a creative force that was in all forms of life and felt he had a mission to express this in his work. He used *vibrant* colours and agitated brushwork to express his deep emotions. In his **Self-Portrait** of 1889 his *luminous* head with burning eyes is set against a whirlpool of darkness and he wrote, 'I want to paint men and women with that something of the eternal which the halo used to symbolise'.

In a different way, **Cézanne** also expressed his own personal experience of the world around him. He had decided 'to make of Impressionism something solid and *durable*, like the art of the museums'. He believed everything in nature could be described by the basic forms of the cone, the sphere and the cylinder. He wanted to organise his experience of the world and every brushstroke was like a building block in his search for a composition with a strong structure and a pleasing combination of form and colour. In his final years, he achieved his aim in his pictures of the mountain, **Mont Sainte-Victoire** (1904–1906) (see page 52).

What did the Post-Impressionists like to paint and what methods did they use?

In the same way as the aims of the four major Post-Impressionist artists were different from each other, so too were their methods. Artists who came after them were often influenced by the technique and style of more than one of these artists and so their work as a group has provided a rich body of knowledge and experimentation. Their methods were as follows:

Georges Seurat (1869–1891)

- Wanted to bring more structure into his work and studied scientific theories of colour and light.

- Did not want to work straight from nature in the unplanned way of the Impressionists. Instead he studied *classical* painters and made lots of studies before he made his final painting.

- Pioneered a new way of working which was called *Pointillism*, *Divisionism* or *Neo-Impressionism*. He built up his paintings with criss-cross brushstrokes and dots of pure colour which created an overall glow of light.

Amongst the artists who developed *Divisionism* with Seurat were **Paul Signac** (1863–1935) and **Camille Pissarro** (1830–1903).

- Pissarro tried to combine the Impressionists' skill at creating atmosphere with the detailed technique of the *Divisionists*. In this way he created a beautiful image of a foggy river called **Ile Lacrois, Rouen**, 1888.

- Signac loved the sea and in his painting of **The Côte d'Azur**, 1889 (see page 8) he created a strong sense of mood using small dots of paint. After Seurat's death, he opened up the *Pointillist* technique and used bold dashes of *vibrant* colour as in **The Fort St. Jean, Marseille**, 1907.

classical – following the rules of art first set out in ancient Greece and Rome.

Ile Lacrois, Rouen (1888) by Camille Pissarro
John G. Johnson Collection, Philadelphia Museum of Art

Paul Gauguin (1848–1903)

- Made a bold move away from the Impressionist style and used colour and form in a *symbolic* way to express an inner world of feeling.
- Painted bold flat areas of colour inside black outlines which was called the *Cloissonnist* style and was based on stained glass *enamelling*.
- Was the leader of the *Synthetic Symbolists* who wanted the *symbolic* power of paintings to be expressed through colour and form alone and not by referring to literature or mythology.

A young artist who joined Gauguin in Brittany was:

- **Paul Serusier**, (1864–1927). Serusier painted a local beauty spot called the Bois d'Amour, under Gauguin's direction. His circle of friends in Paris named the painting **The Talisman**, 1888 (see page 39), and it formed the basis of their ideas about the importance of colour over content.
- The young painters formed a group called the *Nabis* which had in it, **Maurice Denis** (1870–1943), **Edouard Vuillard** (1868–1940) and **Pierre Bonnard** (1867–1947).
- Maurice Denis made the statement, '*A picture – before being a war horse, a female nude, or some anecdote – is essentially a flat surface covered with colours in a particular order*', and this was to become one of the most important ideas for 20th century painters.
- Vuillard was one of the most gifted of the *Nabis* painters. He combined Gauguin's designs of flat areas of colour with the shimmering *Divisionist* technique of Seurat to produce private scenes of his family and friends at home, like **A Family Evening** of 1895 (see page 9).
- From 1891, Paul Gauguin mainly lived on the island of Tahiti in the South Seas. In his work he used flattened *perspective*, unrealistic and *symbolic* colour and patterned space. His earlier paintings are more brightly coloured visions of an earthly paradise whilst his later paintings are more dreamlike and have a darker mood.

Cloissonism – a style of painting developed by Paul Gauguin which was based on medieval stained glass windows and enamels. He painted thick black lines around areas of bright colour.

enamelling – a method of decorating metal which results in a brightly coloured, glass-like surface.

symbol / symbolic – a sign or object which stands in for, and refers to, a hidden or deeper meaning.

Vincent Van Gogh (1853–1890)

- In 1886, when Van Gogh saw the work of the Impressionist painters in Paris, he started using brighter colours and experimented with the *Divisionist* ideas of Seurat.

- He expressed the main message of his paintings through his *vibrant* (rich) colour combinations. He used swirling and lively brushwork to create a feeling of nervous energy and *spiritual intensity*.

- His vibrant colour and expressive line and brushwork inspired a new generation of **Expressionist** artists.

Paul Cézanne (1839–1906)

- Learnt a lot about the use of colour and light from the Impressionist painter, **Camille Pissarro**. However, Cézanne worried that the effects of light made things look less solid and wanted to have more structure in his work. He wanted his paintings to be more truthful to the way we *perceive* things and understand our experience of the world.

- Worked straight from the landscape and carefully studied its structure. He developed a new way of building up compositions using patches of colour (**Landscape with Rocks and Trees**, 1880–1885).

- The surface of his pictures are made up of blocks of colour put on the canvas with directional brushstrokes or smeared on thickly with a palette knife. His pictures are real landscapes and *abstract* compositions at the same time.

- He gets a sense of depth by putting colours side by side in *harmonious* combinations rather than using *perspective* drawing and tonal shading.

Many great masters of the 20th century were influenced by **Cézanne**'s work including **Henri Matisse** and **Pablo Picasso** and the *Cubists*.

vibrant – vivid, thrilling.

spiritual – involving the inner, expressive side of human understanding.

intensity – a depth or strength of feeling which is almost too much to take.

perception / perceive – the way we directly understand the world through the senses such as seeing and touching, and our thought.

harmony / harmonious – being in agreement and peaceful.

perspective – a way of constructing a picture from a particular viewpoint as though you were looking through a window into it.

Landscape with Rocks and Trees (1880–1885) by Paul Cézanne
Philadelphia Museum of Art: The Louise and Walter Arensberg Collection, 1950

Biographies of Artists and their Paintings Explored

PART
TWO

Portrait of Seurat (1883)
by Ernest Laurent
Louvre, D.A.G. (fonds Orsay)

Born: 2nd December 1859
Died: 29th March 1891
Place of Birth: Paris, France
Family details: His father was a legal official and his
mother was the daughter of a Paris jeweller. Seurat
was the third of four children. He had two brothers
and a sister.
Paintings analysed:
Bathers at Asnières, 1884
The Circus, 1891

GEORGES SEURAT

Childhood

Georges Pierre Seurat was born on 2nd December, 1859. When he was a young boy his uncle taught him how to draw and paint and he became a skilful artist at an early age.

Youth

At 16, he went to drawing classes at college and was very excited about reading a book called *Grammaire des Arts du Dessin* by the art historian, **Charles Blanc** which explained all his latest ideas on drawing and painting.

In 1878, Seurat went to the School of Fine Art in Paris (Ecole des Beaux-Arts). He studied the Old Masters including the French *classical* painter, **Auguste Ingres**. He also read a new book by **David Sutter** on the Phenomena of Vision. This book together with the colour theories of **Eugene Chevreul** (*Law of Simultaneous Contrast*, 1839) and **Ogden Rood** (*Modern Chromatics*, 1879) helped Seurat to plan his own theories about the use of colour and tone.

The Sacred Wood, Cherished by the Arts and the Muses (1884–1889) by Pierre Puvis de Chavannes
Art Institute of Chicago, IL, USA

Development of his artistic career

In the early 1880s, Seurat went on lots of sketching trips into the suburbs of Paris. The charcoal drawing of the 24-year-old Seurat shows him as a sensitive young man who is keen to do well (**Portrait of Seurat**, 1883, by **Ernest Laurent**) (see page 16). In 1883 he began his first large canvas called **Bathers at Asnières**, 1883–1884 (see page 22), and in the same year he also had his *conte* drawing of his friend **Aman-Jean** accepted at the major art Exhibition in Paris, the Salon.

In 1884, Seurat's **Bathers** was rejected by the Salon and he showed it instead in an exhibition held by the Société des Artistes Indépendants. Here **Paul Signac** and other artists admired his work and were influenced by his new ideas on colour and light. Seurat and Signac worked on a new technique of painting which was given the name *Divisionism* or *Pointillism*.

conte – compressed charcoal.

A Sunday Afternoon on the Island
of La Grande Jatte (1884–1886)
by Georges Seurat
Art Institute of Chicago, IL, USA

A Sunday Afternoon on the Island of La Grande Jatte, 1884–1886

In 1886, Seurat showed his second great canvas at the eighth and final Impressionist Exhibition. It was called **A Sunday Afternoon on the Island of La Grande Jatte** and was the first example of Seurat's mature *Pointillist* style. In it he covered the canvas with dots of pure colour which he wanted viewers to mix *optically* into new colours when they stood back and looked at it.

The composition of **La Grande Jatte** was carefully planned out and the figures look still and *monumental*. This painting is crowded with lots of different people from soldiers to grandmothers and small babies – but they all look very still as if they are frozen in time. Some people said they were arranged across the painting like a *classical frieze* on an ancient Greek temple. It showed how much Seurat admired fresco painters like his friend **Puvis de Chavannes (The Sacred Wood, Cherished by the Arts and the Muses**, 1884–1889) (see page 18). Sadly, most of the critics did not like Seurat's work and only the journalist Felix Feneon wrote an article in *Vogue* praising his painting and saying it was the beginning of the new style of *Neo-Impressionism*.

optically – visually, relating to the eye and how we see.

monumental – an art object that is usually massive, permanent and imposing.

Leader of the Neo-Impressionists

Seurat was fast becoming the leader of a new school of Neo-Impressionist painters, which had in it well-known artists like **Camille Pissarro** and **Paul Signac**. He also inspired other groups to follow his way of painting and, in 1886, he exhibited seven paintings with a new Belgian group of painters called *Les Vingt* (The Twenty) which was a big success.

The art critic, **Felix Feneon**, went on supporting Seurat's work and introduced him to the young mathematician, Charles Henry, who worked on the theory behind art. Seurat put Henry's ideas on the emotional effect of line and colour into his paintings and completed **Les Poseuses** (The Models) and **Invitation to the Sideshow** between 1887 and 1888.

Despite critics in Paris not liking his work, Seurat went on working keenly and between 1889 and 1890 he completed **Le Chahut** (The Can-Can) and **Young Woman Powdering Herself**. He also produced studies of café night-life and paintings of the town of Honfleur on the French coast.

In his personal life he had met the model, Madeleine Knobloch, who was the subject of the painting **Young Woman Powdering Herself**, and she gave birth to their son in February, 1890.

Le Chahut (c.1889)
by Georges Seurat
Samuel Courtauld Trust, Courtauld Institute of Art Gallery

Les Poseuses/The Models (1888) by Georges Seurat
Private Collection

Seurat wanted his pictures to be more *monumental* then the Impressionists.

The end of Seurat's career

In 1891, Seurat had another successful exhibition with the **Les Vingt** group in Belgium and worked on a large painting of **The Circus**. Seurat was so pleased with this painting and keen to have it seen that he exhibited it in an unfinished state at the *Salon des Indépendants* on 16th March, 1891. Many critics praised its 'undulating music of lines' and 'powerful impression of radiant pleasure'.

Seurat seemed to be at the top of his career but sadly tragedy struck. Less than two weeks after he showed **The Circus** (see page 24) Seurat was suddenly taken ill and died on the 29th March, 1891. He had been struck down by either meningitis or diptheria. His little son died shortly after of the same infection.

With Seurat's sudden death, the Neo-Impressionist painters lost the main person in their group. Slowly, they gave up Seurat's scientific method of painting and developed their own personal variations of the *Pointillist* style.

Despite Seurat's early death he still had a big influence on future generations. The *Futurists* in Italy; **Picasso**, **Delaunay** and the *Cubists*; and **Naum Gabo** and the *Constructivists*, all admired his work and the way he had tried to bring together new scientific theories and the latest developments in art.

Bal au Moulin Rouge (1889)
by Jules Cheret
Private Collection

The colours and designs in Cheret's posters were a strong influence on Seurat's painting of the circus, 1891.

Bathers at Asnières, 1884, by Georges Seurat

National Gallery, London, UK

Background

Bathers at Asnières, 1884, was shown at the Salon des Indépendants in 1884 after being rejected by the *Salon* jury. In contrast to the small-scale works of *Impressionism*, Seurat's painting was monumental, 3 metres wide and 2 metres high. It showed a popular subject of Impressionist painting – people relaxing by the River Seine – but it was painted in a new and challenging way, showing both what Seurat had learnt from classical art and his understanding of modern scientific ideas.

Seurat's scene has lost the snapshot effect of Impressionist art and has a still and timeless quality. Unlike the Impressionists, Seurat made many sketches before planning this large composition. This was the start of his painting technique called *Divisionism* or *Pointillism* because of the way the tiny dots of paint created a beautiful glow of colour and light when viewed from afar.

He developed this technique more fully in a large painting which went with the **Bathers** called **La Grande Jatte**, 1884–1886 (see page 19) a smart, popular leisure spot.

His way of working inspired other artists like **Pissarro** and **Signac**.

Ideas

- Set up a still life in sunlight and paint it in the *Pointillist* technique. Take care to put dots of paint to show the actual colours of the objects, then add orange for the sunlight, then reflected colours from neighbouring objects and, lastly, all the *complementary colours*. Take your time over it and make sure you get the right balance of colours so that when you stand back from your work your eye *optically* mixes the colours you want to see.

- Look through a magnifying glass at the coloured areas in old comics or magazines. You will find out that, in the printing process, tiny dots of colour are put side by side to make up new colours. Seurat loved popular prints and posters and in the 1960s Pop artists such as Andy Warhol and Roy Lichtenstein became very interested in the colour effects that were achieved in comics and magazines. Try looking at some of their work too.

radiate – to shine out in all directions.

frieze – horizontal broad band of sculpture at the top of a Greek temple or other work of art.

Form

The composition is balanced and *symmetrical*. The line of the riverbank takes your eye through to the background and the figures are evenly spaced along it. The trees on either side of the river balance each other. The white sails of the boats also mirror each other on either side of the river.

The riverbanks are joined by the bridge and factory buildings. The pillars under the bridge and the factory chimneys are evenly spaced across the back of the picture. They look like columns on a *classical* temple.

Seurat admired artists who worked in the classical tradition and made copies of the work of the classical French painter, **Ingres**. He also loved the clear colours and balanced compositions of the 15th century Italian artist, **Pierro della Francesco** whose work has the same silent atmosphere as Seurat's paintings.

Process

Seurat created a technique called '*optical* painting' which makes a glow of light and colour across the picture. He used criss-cross brushstrokes underneath and dots of paint on top.

'*Optical* painting' was a long, hard process. To paint the river water, Seurat first put on dots of blue and green for the water and then added pale orange for sunlight. Next he added colours for reflections of the sky and other objects, and lastly the complementary colours of everything around. Each layer of paint had to dry before a new layer was added so the colours did not become mixed but stayed pure and bright. Our own eyes mix and blend the colours when we stand back to look at the picture.

Seurat studied scientific theories of colour as in Eugene Chevreul's book about complementary opposites. He was also a master of tone as you can see in his black *conte* sketch of the **Seated Boy with a Straw Hat**. This shows how well he understood the use of light and dark shading.

In his paintings, Seurat used the same effects of contrasting tone as in his black and white drawings. The boy with a straw hat is wearing a dark blue top which contrasts with the lighter colours of the sand and the pale yellow dots in the grass.

Content

Although at first glance **Bathers at Asnières** shows an ordinary group of people relaxing by the river, when we take a closer look we realise the figures are all male. In fact, this is probably the lunchbreak for some of the workers in the new *urban* industries. In the distance Seurat has put in the smoking chimneys of some of these newly built factories.

Seurat felt sorry for the working classes and had close friends in the *Anarchist* and *Communist* groups which hoped to see changes come about in their living and working conditions. *Anarchists* stressed the need for everyone to enjoy leisure time not just the middle classes. They believed in using technology and industry in such a way that everyone could enjoy free time.

Therefore, this painting shows an odd and rather shocking subject. Most Impressionist paintings showed middle-class day trippers enjoying themselves in suburban resorts like Argenteuil or Grenouillére. In fact, the boat heading for the far bank is carrying a well-dressed couple across to La Grande Jatte for a day out, but the woman is sitting with her back and parasol turned firmly away from the little group on the bank.

Mood

Unlike paintings by Impressionist painters like Renoir, in which people enjoy chatting together and dancing, Seurat's painting creates an atmosphere of silence and stillness. There is not much communication between the people sitting on the bank and the main figure lies with his back to us gazing into the distance, lost in his own thoughts.

There is a haze of light which glows throughout the whole painting. This *luminous* quality creates a rather eerie or magical effect. Everything seems strangely quiet and calm and the people sit motionless on the bank whilst a boat glides past on the river.

The Circus, 1891, by Georges Seurat

Musee d'Orsay, Paris, France

tranquility – calm, peacefulness.

optically – visually, relating to the eye and how we see.

caricatures – a way of sketching a person which is over-done and often grotesque.

anonymous – nameless and unknown.

Background

Paris night life had been a favourite Impressionist subject. Cafés often had bands, singers and dancers. **Manet** painted a café-concert in **The Waitress**, 1878–1879, and **Degas** was fascinated by the effects of artificial lighting in **Café Singer**, 1878.

Seurat often visited Concert Européen and L'Ancien Monde in Montmartre, Paris. The shows ended with an exciting, noisy act, the fashionable can-can dance or 'le Chahut'. In 1889–1890 Seurat painted **Le Chahut**, using all his latest theories on line and tone. But critics thought it was too mechanical and lifeless.

The circus was also popular and Cirque Medrano was not far from Seurat's studio. Artists loved the atmosphere of happiness and danger and Seurat made many studies of the movements of the clowns, dancers and ringmasters.

One year after **Le Chahut** (see page 20), Seurat painted **The Circus** and this was much more of a success. One critic said of it, 'What a powerful impression of radiant pleasure, what an undulating music of lines!'

Ideas

- Try making your own studies of people and animals in movement. Maybe you can visit a travelling circus and make some sketches which you can use back at home to make up an exciting picture.

- Try out some of Charles Henry's theories on line and colour.

- Pale, warm colours = happiness and action
Dark, cool colours = sadness
Upward moving lines = joy
Downward moving lines = sadness

- Middle tones in colour, horizontal and vertical lines = *harmony* and *tranquility*

- Make up your own *compositions* using different directions of line and colour combinations. See how they affect the mood or atmosphere of your work.

Content

Seurat's view of the circus performance shows a female acrobat balancing with one foot on the back of a horse as it gallops around the ring. This was one of the most popular and exciting acts of the Medrano Circus.

Also in the circus ring are clowns who swirl ribbons and perform acrobatic tricks to make the show even more thrilling. The ringmaster cracks his whip to make the horse go through its paces and keep up the speed of the performance.

At the far side of the ring are rows of spectators. The tiers of seats were priced differently, with the cheapest being at the top and the most expensive being the seats with backrests nearest the front. Seurat has made an witty comment about social classes by showing workers in caps, relaxed and leaning over the ballustrade (type of railing) right at the top and the well-dressed middle classes sitting rather stiffly at the front.

Form

Seurat's **Circus** is a very *dynamic* composition, full of movement and excitement. The horse has all four legs off the ground and a yellow ribbon zigzags out behind the dancer. The trainer's whip snakes across the middle of the picture under the horse.

Seurat's composition was inspired by the posters of Jules Cheret posters which advertised popular night-spots in Paris such as the Moulin Rouge. There was a wonderfully free sense of movement in the line drawings of these posters and the colour range was like that used by Seurat in the **Circus**. In Jules Cheret's poster for the **Bal Au Moulin Rouge** there is a dancer on horseback like Seurat's dancer (see page 21).

Seurat admired the ideas of the scientist, Charles Henry, whom he met in 1886. Henry was working on the effect that line, colour and tone had on our emotions and feelings. According to Henry, pale, warm colours showed happiness and action whilst dark, cool colours stood for sadness. Likewise, upward moving lines expressed joy and downward moving lines meant sadness. Middle tones in colour and horizontal and vertical lines stood for *harmony* and *tranquillity*.

Seurat used Henry's theories when he drew the upward body movements of the acrobats, their facial features and the shapes of their head-dresses. Other upward moving lines are the curve of the circus ring, the sweep of the curtain on the right and the swirling ribbon held by the clown in the foreground.

Process

This painting shows Seurat's mature style of *Pointillism* and his understanding of the theories on *optical* mixing described by the American, Ogden Rood in his book called *Modern Chromatics* in 1879.

The picture's impact centres around Seurat's use of the *complementary colours*, orange and blue. Rood's idea of *simultaneous contrast* meant that if a dark block of tone met a lighter one, the tones were both enriched by the contrast.

Seurat uses blue dots for the darker, shaded areas and warm orange dots for the areas lit by gas-light. The figures in the audience are outlined in blue dots which separates them from the background. The area surrounding the clown at the front of the picture is thick with blue dots and this makes him stand out from the sandy coloured circus ring.

Mood

At first sight Seurat's painting of the circus is a happy picture of a thrilling performance. He shows us a slice of Parisian nightlife which was open to everyone in society.

This painting can also be seen to have a more unsettling side because the entertainers' faces look exaggerated and slightly *distorted* like *caricatures*. The *anonymous* crowd of onlookers are rather threatening because they look stiff and many of them stare blankly ahead.

Self Portrait with Felt Hat (1887)
by Vincent Van Gogh

Amsterdam, Van Gogh Museum (Vincent van
Gogh Foundation)

Born: 30th March 1853
Died: 29th July 1890
Place of Birth: Groot-Zundert, Netherlands
Family details: His father was a Calvinist pastor. He
was the eldest of six children.
Paintings analysed:
Van Gogh's Bedroom at Arles, 1889
Wheatfield with Cypresses, 1889

VINCENT VAN GOGH

Childhood

Vincent Van Gogh was born on 30th March, 1853, in a small village in Holland called Groot-Zundert. He was the eldest son of a pastor (vicar) and was very close to his younger brother, Theo. He showed a talent for drawing as young as nine years old.

Early career

social-realist – a realistic style of art which claimed to show the true situation of people in society.

composition – the layout or formal design of a picture.

Van Gogh tried out different jobs when he was a young man such as working for an art dealer called Goupil in Paris and being a teacher in England. He admired Dutch and English landscape artists like **Joseph Turner** and **John Constable**. He also liked artists and writers who wanted to show what life was really like for poor people, so he read novels by the French writer, Emile Zola, and studied paintings like **Applicants for Admission to a Casual Ward**, 1874, by the English *social-realist* painter, **Luke Fildes** (1843–1927).

In 1877, Van Gogh went back to Holland and studied to become a priest like his father. He became a missionary in one of the poor mining towns in Belgium but the harsh conditions of the mining families upset him and he lost his job.

The Potato Eaters (1885) by Vincent Van Gogh
Amsterdam, Van Gogh Museum (Vincent van Gogh Foundation)

At 27 years old, he decided to become a full-time artist. He admired the French painter, **François Millet**, because he showed the life of poor peasants. Van Gogh went to the country area of Brabant and there completed his first major *composition*, **The Potato Eaters**, 1885. In this painting he tried to show the life of a poor peasant family just as it was.

Van Gogh sees the Impressionists in Paris

1886 was a very important year in Van Gogh's career as an artist. He went to study art in Paris and saw the Impressionists' work for the first time. He met **Pissarro**, **Gauguin**, **Seurat** and **Signac** and was fascinated by the colour theories and techniques they were exploring. Van Gogh's work changed rapidly as he took in these new ways of working in colour. His **Self-Portrait with Felt Hat** of 1887, shows himself as a very intense young man surrounded by swirling dashes of bright colours, and **Interior of a Restaurant**, 1887, clearly shows the influence of Seurat's *Pointillist* techniques.

Van Gogh was very keen to use colour to express what he wanted. He learnt a lot from Impressionism and became fascinated by the decoration and *composition* in Japanese prints. He organised an exhibition of Japanese prints in the Café du Tambourin which he often visited with his artist friends. **Agostina Segatori in the Café du Tambourin**, 1887, shows the owner of this café with paintings in the Japanese style on the walls behind her.

Sunflowers (1888)
by Vincent Van Gogh
Neue Pinakothek, Munich, Germany

Agostina Segatori in the Café du Tambourin (1887)
by Vincent Van Gogh
Amsterdam, Van Gogh Museum (Vincent van Gogh Foundation)

The Pink Peach Tree (1888)
by Vincent Van Gogh
Amsterdam, Van Gogh Museum (Vincent van Gogh Foundation)

Van Gogh goes to Arles in the south of France

In May, 1888, Van Gogh left Paris and went to Arles in the south of France. When he first arrived, the peach and apricot trees were in blossom and Van Gogh completed 14 canvases in just one month. He loved the light in the south and his paintings show the influence of the Japanese prints he and his brother Theo had collected in Paris (**The Pink Peach Tree**, 1888).

Van Gogh also wanted to set up a group of artists in the south and he was delighted when **Paul Gauguin** came to stay in 1888. He painted his famous series of **Sunflowers**, 1888 (see page 28) to decorate the walls of Gauguin's room. Sadly, the two artists had bitter arguments over their work and Gauguin finally left just before Christmas. Van Gogh was very upset and had a complete breakdown. He cut off part of his ear and was then taken into the Saint Paul Asylum in Saint-Remy.

Van Gogh stayed as a patient at the hospital for some time but he was able to go on working. He made several paintings in the hospital grounds and did striking portraits of hospital staff and patients. After a while he was able to paint in the landscape nearby and created many memorable pictures of the small town of Saint-Remy and the countryside around it (**Starry Night**, 1889). His style during this period was becoming much more expressive with swirling lines and intense colour combinations.

Starry Night (1889)
by Vincent Van Gogh
Museum of Modern Art (MoMA), New York, USA

Van Gogh goes to Auvers-sur-Oise, just outside Paris

By May, 1889, Van Gogh felt much better and discharged himself from the hospital. He went to Paris and stayed with his brother, Theo, who had always helped Vincent with money. He soon got tired of the noisy city and left again for the small village of Auvers-sur-Oise. There he made good friends with Dr. Gachet who went on with his treatment. In the last months of his life, he produced deeply moving and passionate work such as the **Portrait of Dr Gachet**, June 1890, and **The Church at Auvers**, June, 1890.

Portrait of Dr Gachet (1890)
by Vincent Van Gogh
Private Collection

The Church at Auvers (1890) by Vincent Van Gogh
Musée d'Orsay, Paris

Wheatfield with Crows (1890)
by Vincent Van Gogh
Rijksmuseum Vincent Van Gogh, Amsterdam, The Netherlands

End of his career

Van Gogh was still very anxious about his future. Although many artists admired his work, he had only just sold his first painting at an exhibition of the group called 'Les Vingt' held in Brussels. He did not want to rely on his brother for money who was now married and starting a family.

On 27th July, 1890 Van Gogh tried to commit suicide by shooting himself in the chest. Tragically, he died two days later from his wound. His last paintings are disturbing and show intense emotions. Just before his death, he painted **Wheatfield with Crows**, July, 1890. Some people have seen the black birds flying in across the field as *symbols* of death and the dark blue stormy sky creates a mood of darkness throughout the picture.

Van Gogh's brother, Theo, became ill and died only six months after Vincent. Theo's widow returned to Holland with the collection of Van Gogh's paintings and did her best to make sure he finally got the recognition he deserved. Van Gogh's intense use of colour and expressive line and brushwork inspired a new generation of *Expressionist* artists.

symbol and *symbolic* –
a sign or object which stands in for, and refers to, a hidden or deeper meaning.

*Expressionism /
Expressionist* – a group of artists who believed that the most important thing was them to express their own thoughts and feelings rather than follow traditional rules of art.

Van Gogh's Bedroom at Arles, 1888, by Vincent Van Gogh

Art Institute of Chicago, IL, USA

Ideas

■ Make sketches and take photos of your own bedroom. Put in things which are important to you and tell us something about your life. Think about the viewpoint you are going to do it from. Are you going to show just a corner of the room with your bed in it or try to include more things?

■ Try out the effect of using *complementary colours* in your own painting. You don't have to stick to the colours your bedroom really is. Experiment with the tones as well as the contrasts of colour to create the atmosphere you want. This could be cheerful, gloomy, thoughtful and quiet, and so on.

Background

In February, 1888, Van Gogh ended his two-year stay in Paris and went to Arles in the South of France. He was attracted by the brightness of colour and light in that region and wanted to start up a group of artists there.

In May, Van Gogh rented four rooms in the yellow house which he painted in **The Street**, 1888. The scenery in the south inspired Van Gogh to finish 14 canvases in the first month. These were mainly landscape paintings and views of blossoming peach and apricot trees like **The Pink Orchard**, 1888 (see page 29).

He was very excited about his move and decorated his rooms with paintings. An artist's bedroom was an odd subject for a painting at this time but in October, 1888, Van Gogh began working hard on this picture which was going to be the first of three versions. He wrote to his brother, Theo, saying, '*It is a masterpiece!*'.

Van Gogh looked forward to Gauguin coming to stay and painting with him. He completed many of his famous paintings of **Sunflowers**, 1888, to decorate Gauguin's room. Sadly, Gauguin's visit ended in a quarrel just before Christmas, 1888. Gauguin went back to Paris and Van Gogh had a mental breakdown.

contemplation – deep thought.

distort – to twist or stretch something in to a different shape, to deform it.

harmony / harmonious – being in agreement and peaceful.

optimism – a way of looking at the world in which you only expect good things.

Content

The hectic life of Paris was too much for Van Gogh and he wanted to lead a simple life amongst ordinary people in the little town of Arles. This painting shows the plain and humble room he slept in, but the brightly coloured bed cover and paintings around the walls give it a cheerful feeling, Van Gogh had wanted to become a priest (when he was younger) and this room seems fitting for a religious man.

Van Gogh was poor and his bedroom is quite small with only a few pieces of furniture in it – his wooden bed, two wooden chairs and a table with a washing basin and jug on it. Two portraits hang over the bed and there are pictures of landscapes in plain wooden frames around the room.

Form

The *perspective* of this room is slightly *distorted*. From this angle the floor seems oddly steep. It is as if Van Gogh is looking down at the floor and then up again at the window straight ahead in the same picture. Also, the sides of the room open out at the edges of the picture which make you feel you are there in Van Gogh's bedroom yourself.

Van Gogh wrote to his brother, '*This time it's just simply my bedroom, only here colour is to do everything*'. Van Gogh arranged his picture into large blocks of colour. He also created a *vibrant* effect by contrasting *complementary colours* such as blue/orange and red/green.

The orange wooden bed makes a striking contrast with the blue walls and doors behind. The large area of the floor is mainly green with patches of reddy brown on the bare boards. These colours are picked up again in the window in the back wall. The bright red blanket also stands out as a bold patch of rich colour against the green of the floor.

Process

Van Gogh uses various brushwork techniques to create effects of texture. The curved brushstrokes on the pillows make them look soft to the touch. The appearance of wicker work on the seats of the chairs is created by overlaying lots of long, thin brushstrokes. The wooden floorboards are painted in long dashes of thick paint which are dragged across the surface of the canvas to give a rough effect.

The colour theme of complementary opposites is taken through the whole painting. The yellowy orange chairs stand out against the blue background and Van Gogh has brushed streaks of yellow into the blue door. A pale yellow towel is hanging on the blue wall. These colour contrasts do not jar because the tones of the colours are similar – the blue has been mixed with white to bring it closer to the naturally lighter tone of the yellow.

In some areas Van Gogh blends *complementary colours* together and this also brings a sense of unity into the picture. There are patches on the floor where the complementary opposites of green and red are mixed together to create softer tones which make the overall effect more *harmonious*.

Mood

This painting has a personal and intimate mood. We feel we can in some way experience what Van Gogh's life was like and what it was like being him. It is like a self-portrait of the painter and we feel we can get closer to the man himself.

Van Gogh suffered a lot from depression but this painting of his bedroom was painted in a productive and happier time in his life. It shows a simple existence but one which is focused on the creative life of painting. It gives a feeling of *optimism* as well as *contemplation*.

There is a hint of loneliness in the display of the two portraits above his bed. One is a self-portrait and one is of a woman. We are reminded of Van Gogh's failed relationships with women and his ongoing search for love.

Wheatfield with Cypresses, 1889, by Vincent Van Gogh

National Gallery, London, UK

Background

Van Gogh had a very emotional and intense personality and when, after a fierce argument, Paul Gauguin left Arles in December, 1888, Van Gogh suffered a mental breakdown.

Early in 1889, Van Gogh had himself taken into the nearby Asylum de St. Paul in St. Remy-en-Provence. Luckily, he was able to go on working and painted portraits and views of the grounds of the hospital. **The Garden of Saint-Paul Hospital**, 1889, shows the side of the hospital and the garden enclosed by a wall.

At the hospital Van Gogh lived the quiet life of a monk and found expression for his feelings, fears and beliefs in his art. His paintings often have darker and more gloomy colours than those painted earlier at Arles but the main development is his swirling and flickering brushwork. The way he puts on the paint shows his mental restlessness and the depth of his emotional response to nature.

In June, 1889, Van Gogh completed **Wheat Field with Cypresses at the Haute Galline near Eygalieres**. As the golden **Sunflowers**, 1888, had been one of his favourite subjects in happier times at Arles, now the dark Cypress trees which dominated the landscape at Saint-Remy were chosen by Van Gogh to express his troubled inner feelings.

Ideas

- Create a variety of textures and effects by experimenting with different kinds of brushstrokes. You can use streaky, curved, feathery, dashed and dabbed brushwork. You can work *wet-in-wet* or build up layers of dried paint.

- Go to a park or out into the countryside and take time to choose an interesting viewpoint or composition. Keep it simple like Van Gogh did. Then use your experiments with brushwork techniques to create a dramatic effect in your painting. Make sure everything in your painting looks full of life and nervous energy.

wet-in-wet – a painting technique in which the artist does not allow the first layer of paint to dry before adding more paint, usually in a different colour on top.

spiritual – involving the inner, expressive side of human understanding.

symbol and *symbolic* – a sign or object which stands in for, and refers to, a hidden or deeper meaning.

Content

Van Gogh was a genius at producing a striking and dramatic effect out of a simple composition. His view of the landscape around Saint-Remy is dominated by the swirling sky and the towering Cypress trees on the right of the picture.

There is a range of blue hills, called the Alpilles, in the distance and a golden field of ripe wheat in the foreground. Grass and poppies are sketched in at the edge of the field.

The whole painting is created in swirling and lively brushstrokes which express Van Gogh's intense state of mind at this time. In the same month Van Gogh also painted one of his most famous pictures, **Starry Night**, June, 1889 (see page 29). The dark silhouette of the Cypress tree again dominates the picture. The little town of Saint-Remy has olive groves and mountains all around it and the night-time sky is filled with spinning flashes of light. The church spire as well as the dark cypress tree stretches up into the fantastic *luminous* glow created by Van Gogh's whirling brushstrokes.

Form

In this painting, Van Gogh has transformed a simple view of a field with shrubs and trees into a powerful, dramatic composition. The picture is built up on three strong diagonals which create a zigzag formation across the picture.

The diagonal in the background is formed by a range of blue hills which sweep from right to left. The rolling shapes of the hills are echoed in the sweeping curves of the clouds in the sky.

The edges of the field create two more diagonals which enclose the windswept wheat. The Cypress tree is painted like a huge, dark flame that reaches up into the sky. The shrubs are painted with feathery brushstrokes which make them look like strange creatures given life from within.

Process

Van Gogh has built his painting around the striking contrast between the blue of the sky and mountains with the orange of the wheatfield. He has also used different types of brushstroke for each of these areas.

The wheatfield is built up of lots of different shades of yellow and orange. The paint is put on in dabs and dashes to suggest the ripe seed heads. The long brushstrokes at the edge of the field describe the direction of the wind in the waving wheat.

The sky is filled with swirling shapes painted 'wet in wet' in turquoise blues, greens and white. The dark shapes of the Cypress trees reach up from the field's edge to the top of the painting. The towering tree is made up of streaky brushwork of different shades of green.

Mood

This landscape is alive with nervous energy. It seems to represent the painter's troubled mind and emotions and his inspired belief in the *spiritual* power of nature.

The dark, gloomy tones of the tall Cypress trees are foreboding. Yet, at the same time, they are full of life and look like flames leaping up into the sky. They seem to symbolise two powerful forces at the same time – light and darkness, life and death, sunlit cheer and black gloom.

The whole of this landscape is worked into with energetic and expressive brushstrokes. This, together with the dark *symbolic* Cypress trees, stands for the disturbed inner life and feelings of Van Gogh's tortured mind.

Self Portrait with Yellow Christ
(1889) by Paul Gauguin
Musée d'Orsay, Paris, France

Born: 7th June 1848
Died: 8th May 1903
Place of Birth: Paris
Family details: His father was a political journalist. He had one older sister.
Paintings analysed:
The Vision after the Sermon, 1888
Te Reroia (Daydreaming), 1897

PAUL GAUGUIN

Childhood

Paul Gauguin was born in Paris on 7th June, 1848. His mother came from a Spanish family who had settled in Peru in South America.

Revolution broke out in France during 1848 and, soon after, his parents decided to take Gauguin and his older sister to make a new life with their relatives in Peru. Tragically, Gauguin's father died on the long sea-journey and the family ended up living with relatives in the capital city of Lima until they returned to France in 1855. Gauguin was then seven years old and his early experiences and memories of living in a hot and exotic country had a lasting influence on him.

Youth and early career

When Gauguin was seventeen he joined the Merchant Navy and sailed to South America again. Gauguin loved travelling and two years later he went into the regular French Navy and spent his time sailing around the world.

Sadly, Gauguin's mother had died in 1867 and his sister had married and emigrated, so when he finally returned to Paris he had no close family left in France. He was able to find work with a firm of stockbrokers where he made friends with **Emile Schuffenecker** who was also a skilled painter. The two men visited nearby art galleries together and this inspired Gauguin to start painting himself. In 1873 he met and married a Danish girl called Mette Sophie Gaad with whom he had four children.

Through his friend Schuffenecker, he met the *Impressionist* painter **Camille Pissarro** who taught and encouraged Gauguin. In 1876, his painting **Landscape at Viroflay** was accepted by the Salon. In 1880 he rented his own studio and exhibited seven paintings at the fifth Impressionist Exhibition. He continued to work using Impressionist techniques and exhibited in 1881 and 1882.

Up until this time Gauguin had been able to support his growing family and his painting career by his work in the stockmarket. At the end of 1882, disaster struck with the collapse of the French economy and Gauguin lost his job in January, 1883. He tried to support his family through his painting, but the few paintings he managed to sell, brought in very little money. In the end, he and his family moved to his wife's home country of Denmark to live with her relatives. Gauguin tried to support them by working as a salesman for a textile firm but in the end he gave up and went back to Paris in 1886.

Development of his career as an artist

Gauguin was now 38 years old and was searching for his own style in painting. He was attracted to the poor, rural area of Brittany in Northern France where the country folk still wore *traditional* costumes and followed simple lives.

Gauguin worked hard and at the final Impressionist Exhibition in 1886 he exhibited 19 paintings based on his trip to Brittany. He started travelling again and visited the French island of Martinique in the Caribbean where he developed his use of bright colours and simple compositions in paintings such as **At the Pond**, 1887.

traditional – a tried and tested way of doing things which is often handed down from one generation to another.

Cloissonism – a style of painting developed by Paul Gauguin which was based on medieval stained glass windows and enamels. He painted thick black lines around areas of bright colour.

medieval – belonging to the Middle Ages which started around the 11th century and finished in the 15th century.

Symbolist manifesto – a written statement of the aims and ideas of Symbolism.

The Talisman (1888)
by Paul Serusier
Musée d'Orsay, Paris, France

Beginning of a new style of painting

After a few months he returned to France and went to Brittany again. It was here that he made one of the most important breakthroughs in his painting style. Together with the painter, **Emile Bernard**, he developed a style which they called *Cloissonism* after the name of a *medieval* enamelling technique which they both admired.

In 1888 Gauguin completed his most successful painting of this period, **Vision after the Sermon (Jacob and the Angel)**, 1888 (see page 42). It was displayed in an exhibition called *The Impressionist and Synthetist Group* at the Café Volpini in the big Universal Exhibition which took place in Paris in 1889 (see top of page 10). Although the Volpini exhibition was mostly ignored by the critics, it did set up Gauguin as the leader of the group of painters who worked in Pont-Aven in Brittany. He had also had a one-man exhibition in 1888 organised by Theo, the brother of Van Gogh, and in 1889 had exhibited 12 paintings with the Les Vingt group of painters in Brussels.

One of the young painters who came under Gauguin's influence was **Paul Serusier**. Under Gauguin's guidance Serusier made a painting which was later to become very famous called **The Talisman**. Serusier admired the way Gauguin used colour in a *symbolic* and emotional way and shared Gauguin's ideas with a group of writers and poets in Paris who had published the *Symbolist Manifesto* in 1886.

By 1891, Gauguin was the leading artist of the *Symbolist* movement. After he left Tahiti, his follower, **Paul Serusier**, continued his influence by forming his artist friends into a group called the *Nabis*. These painters included **Maurice Denis**, **Pierre Bonnard** and **Edouard Vuillard** who were to become well-known figures in the European art world (see page 9).

Life and career on the island of Tahiti

In April, 1891, Gauguin left for Tahiti where he hoped to find an island paradise where the natives lived simple lives in tune with nature and their religion. Sadly, he was disappointed to find that much of the Tahitian religion and lifestyle had already been swept aside by the *colonialists*. Nevertheless, he went to live in a remote spot on the island and there created some wondeful paintings and wrote a book called *Noa, Noa*.

However, despite wanting to discover a new way of life in an earthly paradise, his paintings were always aimed at the European market. He hoped his colourful visions of an exotic world, such as **Joyeuseté**, 1892, and **Her Name is Vairaumati**, 1892, would appeal to people in Paris with their promise of an escape from Western Industrialised society.

Unhappily, during his lifetime Gauguin's work did not find the market he had hoped for and he spent much of his time both poor and ill. In 1893, he returned to France and the collector Durand-Ruel organised an exhibition of 38 paintings from Tahiti, six from Brittany and two sculptures. Sadly, very little sold but Gauguin had become a legendary figure in the artistic world of Paris.

In December, 1894, Gauguin decided to leave France once and for all and organised a sale to fund his journey. The sale only raised 3,000 francs but Gauguin returned to Tahiti anyway.

Early in 1897 his health was so bad that he was taken into hospital. In May of the same year he heard from his wife, Mette, that his only daughter, Aline, had died of pneumonia. Gauguin became very depressed and it was at this point he painted his large mural called **Where do we come from? What are we? Where are we going?**, 1897 (see page 41). The following year he tried to commit suicide and was taken into hospital again.

Joyeuseté (1892) by Paul Gauguin
Musée d'Orsay, Paris, France

Her Name is Vairaumati (1892) by Paul Gauguin
Pushkin Museum, Moscow, Russia

colonialist and colonies – when the government of one country takes over and settles in other lands. Tahiti was a French colony.

Where do we come from? What are we? Where are we going? (1897) by Paul Gauguin
Museum of Fine Arts, Boston, Massachusetts, USA, Tompkins Collection

End of his career

Towards the end of his life Gauguin tried to earn more money by taking a job in the local government on the island. He got into trouble with the authorities when he protested about the treatment of the native population. In 1901, he was about to return again to France but was persuaded not to because his paintings were beginning to sell and dealers thought Gauguin's wild appearance and odd life-style would put people off buying his work.

Gauguin moved to the Marquesas islands in the hopes of starting a new phase of his life. He wanted to live more cheaply and not be bothered by the authorities. However, it was not to be, and in 1902 he was accused of stirring up native revolt and was sentenced to three months in prison. He planned to appeal against this judgement but sadly he became ill and he died on the 8th May, 1903 at the age of 55.

In 1885 Gauguin wrote, '*Above all don't sweat over pictures; a great emotion can be transplanted immediately; dream over it and look for its simplest form*'. Although Gauguin did not make money in his lifetime, he inspired generations of painters that followed, including **Henri Matisse** and the *Fauves* and the German *Expressionist* painters.

The Vision after the Sermon, 1888, by Paul Gauguin

National Gallery of Scotland, Edinburgh, Scotland

Ideas

- Look at stained glass windows and try making up your own composition using bold, dark outlines and bright colours.

- Draw some of your friends using simple shapes so they look like they are carved out of wood.

- Divide your paper with a diagonal line across the middle. Draw some of your friends in the bottom left half of your paper. On the top right side, draw something from your imagination, fantasy or myth. Colour the whole picture in with one bright colour as the background.

Background

In 1888, Gauguin went to Brittany, north-west France. Emile Bernard, a young painter, was working with a small group of artists in the village of Pont-Aven.

Bernard knew about the new artistic ideas in Paris and was influenced by the work of *Symbolist* poets like Stephane Mallarme. He and Gauguin experimented with different ways of expressing *Synthetic Symbolist* ideas through colour and form. Together they developed a new style, *Cloissonism*.

Bernard painted peasants leaving church in **Breton Women in a Green Pasture**, 1888. He outlined each figure in black so that the coloured areas were separated, producing an abstract pattern. Bernard hoped this created a vision of a mystical world beyond everyday life.

Bernard's picture inspired Gauguin to paint the famous, **Vision after the Sermon**. The critics thought Gauguin had created the new style by himself. Bernard was sure that Gauguin had stolen his idea and never forgave him.

impasto – to build paint up on the canvas in very thick layers.

primitive – term given by Europeans to ancient societies in countries like Africa and South America. They thought these societies lived closer to nature and still had ancient customs and tribal rituals.

Content

A group of Breton peasant women fill the front and left-hand side of the painting. They are dressed in *traditional* costume with large white bonnets.

Whilst the women pray devoutly, their faces glow with the light from an unearthly vision.

In the top right-hand corner you can see an angel with outstretched wings struggling with the figure of Jacob from the Bible. Dramatic struggles like this were often shown in early Christian art.

The vision can be seen on the other side of a tree which passes diagonally across the picture, cutting it in half. It creates an artificial division between the real world and that of mystical visions and religious faith. In this way Gauguin mixes an everyday scene of women leaving church with a supernatural one. He loved the peasants' simple life and their deep belief in God.

Form

In this picture, Gauguin successfully combined many of his artistic interests. These were early *medieval* Christian art, folk art, and Japanese prints.

The tree creates a strong diagonal which divides Gauguin's picture into two parts. Japanese woodcut prints were very popular amongst artists at this time and often had designs like this.

Gauguin loved Breton folk art and admired its directness. He drew his peasant women in simple shapes as if they were carved from wood.

The bold shapes of their white bonnets are repeated across the front of the painting. They are outlined in black and stand out against the red background and the black of their costumes. Instead of modelling and *perspective* Gauguin has used flat, simplified shapes which create a bold surface pattern. He has used all his artistic knowledge to create a bold composition of simple forms.

Process

This picture was created in the new style that Bernard and Gauguin worked on together called *Cloissonism*. It was inspired by the *medieval* technique of enamelling as well as stained glass windows. Areas of colour were separated from each other by heavy black outlines and form a pattern across the surface of the painting.

Gauguin was interested in the expressive qualities of shape, line and colour. He used the unnatural bright red background colour for its intense emotional and *symbolic* impact.

Gauguin painted flatly showing few brushstrokes and little texture. In 1888, when he visited Vincent Van Gogh at Arles in the South of France, they argued over technique and style. Gauguin strongly criticised Van Gogh commenting, 'He is a Romantic while my preferences lie with primitive art. When he applies paint he loves the chance effects of *impasto*, but I for my part detest disorderly workmanship'.

Mood

Gauguin created an intense and visionary atmosphere in this painting. The peasant women appear to be in a trance-like state and glow with their intense religious devotion.

Although Gauguin admired the *primitive* in art, this painting is full of all kinds of artistic influences and ideas. Gauguin succeeded in bringing them all together in a powerful composition of bold forms and strong colours.

Te Reroia (Daydreaming), 1897, by Paul Gauguin

Samuel Courtauld Trust, Courtauld Institute of Art Gallery

Ideas

- Create your own version of a dream-like room. You can put in some of the things that meant a lot to you when you were younger. You can include pictures on the walls of childhood memories.

- Make a picture with a view through a window or open door. Try out ways of contrasting the brighter colours of the world outside the room with the softer ones inside. Experiment with the greenish blue and yellow ochre colours Gauguin has used.

- The women look like statues. Their bodies have simple forms in them as though they are carved out of wood. Make up a block of clay and try carving a simple figure out of it.

- Use your clay sculptures as models for a painting. Put them on a piece of patterned material and use dark orange and greenish brown colours to paint their skins to look like they are made out of bronze or wood.

- Experiment with painting on different kinds of surfaces. Note the difference between the effects you can get on rough material and smooth board.

enigmatic – mysterious, hard to understand.

Background

To Gauguin, Western societies were too materialistic. He longed for a more meaningful, natural way of life as did many Symbolists. They wanted to find new ways to express their imagination and experience.

Gauguin was restless. He loved exotic places. He made two trips to Tahiti and lived there between 1891 to 1893 and 1895 to 1903 (see page 40). He tried to recreate Polynesian culture and rituals. He read that Polynesian religion may have had its roots in Egypt and paintings like **We shall not go to market today**, 1892, hint at Egyptian art in the way he has drawn the figures.

In **Joyeuseté**, 1892 (see page 40), he includes Eastern religions, a woman sits in the Buddhist meditation position whilst women in the background worship Buddha or an idol. Gauguin wanted to show Tahiti as an ancient, 'primitive' society at one with nature.

In 1893, Gauguin took his paintings of Tahiti to Paris, but only sold eleven. He was depressed by the response of the public and art critics and went back to Tahiti early in 1895. He painted **Te Reroia** (Daydreaming), in 1897.

Form

In **Te Reroia**, the view through the door behind the women is painted in brighter colours. There is no link between the path in this landscape and the room and this makes the outside world seem far away. The brooding, inward-looking world of dreams inside the room is cut off from the natural world outside.

There is no strongly directed light source in the painting. Light does not flood in from the open doorway behind, but the whole inside scene glows with its own mysterious, atmospheric lighting. The women's bodies seem to have an eerie, *luminous* quality to their skin.

The two women are the main subject of the painting. Gauguin has drawn them in simple shapes, outlined in black, which make them look *monumental* like statues. The greenish-brown colours he has used on their skin make them look like bronze or wooden sculptures. Their heads are thickly painted and stand out against the light golden background.

The people shown in paintings around the walls are drawn in the same simple way. They act out strange scenes which may symbolise ideas and beliefs about the spiritual world.

Content

Many of Gauguin's later paintings are less bright and colourful than the pictures from his first stay on Tahiti. They are often set inside Gauguin's house rather than outside in nature. In **Te Reroia** the colourful view of the natural landscape through the door in the background is very different from the darker colours of the eerily lit inside of the room.

Two women sit silently in the middle of a room while a baby sleeps in its cot. At the bottom of the cot there is a black cushion signed by Gauguin and decorated with a *grotesque* and menacing child-like form.

The walls are decorated with strange scenes which tell dark and threatening stories from the world of dreams and imagination. The women sit together but are lost in their own thoughts. The expression of the woman at the front is *enigmatic* and she seems to question us with her thoughtful and brooding gaze.

Process

Gauguin had little money to spend on paints and equipment. To make savings he started painting on rough, *hessian* fabric but then decided he really liked its coarse, hairy appearance. He thought it added to the effect of the simple, '*primitive*', life that he was trying to show in his pictures. In some places the fabric shows through the thin layers of paint.

Sometimes Gauguin added wax to his paints to thicken them up and create a flatter, smoother surface. The right half of the floor is done in this way and parts of the wall paintings. Gauguin usually put another thin coat of paint over these thicker areas to give the effect of light and tone across the surface.

Gauguin used darker colours inside the room which contrast with the brighter colours in the landscape outside. By contasting dark gold with greenish blue areas he creates an eerie glow.

Mood

The strange unreal light in **Te Reroia** creates a dreamlike atmosphere. In fact, Gauguin wrote to his friend Daniel de Monfried about this painting saying, 'Everything about this picture is dreamlike: is it the dream of the child, the mother, the horseman on the track, or, better still, is it the painter's dream?'

The colours in **Te Reroira** are toned down creating a sad, brooding feeling. The woman sitting cross-legged in a Buddhist pose gazes out at us and we cannot tell what she is thinking.

Around the walls there are painted scenes which may have a strange and dark *Symbolism*. This adds to the unreal and dreamlike mood of the picture.

The small view of the landscape at the back of the picture highlights the unreal, dreamlike atmosphere within the room and contrasts it with the real world outside.

Self-Portrait (1879–1882)
by Paul Cézanne
Pushkin Museum, Moscow, Russia

Born: 19th January 1839
Died: 22nd October 1906
Place of Birth: Aix-en-Provence, South of France
Family details: His father was a successful merchant and banker. He had a sister who was three years younger than him.
Paintings analysed:
Still Life with Basket, 1888–1890
Mont Sainte-Victoire seen from Les Lauves, 1904–1906

PAUL CÉZANNE

Childhood

Cézanne went to the same school as the writer Emile Zola who became famous for his shocking novels about human desire and the life of the poor in the city. Cézanne was a good student who was praised for his achievements in Art as well as Maths, Greek and History.

Youth and early career

Cézanne studied law for three years because his father wanted him to work in the family firm. However, it was clear that Cézanne's real love was painting and his father at last agreed to let him study in Paris.

In 1862, when he was 23, he met many artists, including **Edouard Manet** whose ideas about new directions in art had such a strong influence on younger artists. He also met **Renoir**, **Sisley** and **Pissarro** who later became leading figures in the *Impressionist* movement. These young artists often met at the Café Guerbois to discuss their theories about art and literature. His friend, Zola, and the poets, **Mallarme** and **Baudelaire**, also went there.

The following year, in 1863, Manet's painting called **Déjeuner sur l'Herbe** was rejected by the *Salon* jury along with the work of hundreds of other artists. There were so many complaints that the French Emperor Napoleon III ordered another exhibition to be held of works refused by the Salon. The new exhibition was called the *Salon des Refusés* and Pissarro and Cézanne had paintings displayed in it too.

During the 1860s Cézanne spent his winters in Paris and summers painting in his home town of Aix-en-Provence in the South of France. He was awkward in Paris café society and was well known for his scruffy appearance and rudeness. In 1870, he sent two paintings to be judged by the Salon jury but they were rejected with rude comments.

Salon des Refusés-
exhibition of paintings refused by the Salon.

The Waitress (1878–1879)
by Edouard Manet
Musée d'Orsay, Paris, France

Around this time he met his future wife and two years later they had a son. He left Paris for L'Estaque in the South of France, to avoid being called up to serve in the Army during the Franco-Prussian War. In 1873, he returned and went to live near Pissarro just outside Paris at Auvers. Pissarro was a great influence on Cézanne's work and he encouraged Cézanne to exhibit three paintings at the First Impressionist Exhibition in 1874.

In 1877, he showed 16 paintings at the third Impressionist Exhibition but they were not well thought of by the public or the critics. Cézanne became very fed up and in his **Self-Portrait**, 1879–1882, he looks sad and disappointed. However, his artist friends, like **Pissarro** and **Gauguin**, thought his work was very good and encouraged him to go on painting.

Between 1878 and 1885, Cézanne spent his time moving around France. He concentrated on painting landscapes and made his first painting of the **Mont Sainte-Victoire from the Chemin de Valcros** in 1879, a theme which he was to come back to many times when he was older.

The Card Players (1893–1896)
by Paul Cézanne
Musée d'Orsay, Paris, France

Development of Cézanne's career

Gradually, Cézanne began to get recognition for his work and in 1889 he exhibited with a Belgian group of artists called *Les Vingt* (The Twenty). His paintings were also shown at the 1889 and 1900 World Exhibitions in Paris. Throughout the 1890s he was living in Aix-en-Provence and working enthusiastically on landscapes, still lifes and some portraits. He often made a series of paintings on the same theme such as **The Card Players**, 1893–1896. Other series included **Bathers**, 1902–1906 (see page 48) and **Mont Sainte-Victoire**, 1904–1906.

In 1895, the art dealer, Ambroise Vollard, organised an exhibition of Cézanne's work. This was followed by two more exhibitions of his work in 1898 and 1899, and Cézanne began to enjoy a lot of praise and recognition of his achievement.

In 1900, The Berlin National Gallery became the first museum to buy a painting by Cézanne for their collection. During this period he had several exhibitions in Germany and after 1899 Cézanne took part almost every year in the *Salon des Indépendants*. In 1904 he also exhibited 33 paintings at the *Salon d'Automne*.

Bathers (1902–1906)
by Paul Cézanne
Musée d'Orsay, Paris, France

Salon des Indépendants – exhibitions started in 1884 by Seurat and Signac in opposition to the official Salon.

Salon d'Automne – an exhibition held in the autumn.

End of Cézanne's career

Unluckily, in October, 1906, Cézanne was painting out doors near Aix when he was caught in a thunderstorm and soon became ill with pneumonia. He died several days later on 22nd October, aged 67. In some ways Cézanne was at the peak of his career when he died, he was becoming popular and may have gone on to produce many more masterpieces. Nevertheless, the work he left behind was a great inspiration to many major artists of the 20th century.

Still Life with Basket, 1888–1890, by Paul Cézanne

Musée d'Orsay, Paris, France

Background

Cézanne often painted groups of still life objects in his studio. It is in many of these studies that he developed his new way of describing space and form in painting.

Cézanne was a very slow, *methodical* painter. He sometimes spent days just observing the things he was going to paint. He was keen to record the experience of looking at things and made drawings of the same objects from several angles. In many of his pictures he showed objects from different viewpoints at the same time. He believed that this was closer to the way we saw things as we moved around them.

Cézanne rejected the *traditional* method of using *one-point perspective* to give a sense of depth in his pictures. He created the sense that one object was behind another by using colour alone rather than using perspective drawing. He thought his method of showing where things are in space was more true to our actual experience.

The year after he died, in 1907, there were two big exhibitions of Cézanne's work. Two young painters, **Pablo Picasso** and **Georges Braque** really liked his work. They were fascinated by the way he built up space in his pictures and showed different viewpoints at the same time. Cézanne's work started them on the path to a new way of constructing pictures which was later called *Cubism*.

Ideas

- Make a series of drawings of a small group of fruits. In the first drawing use only outline drawing. In the second drawing use only shading and tone. Compare the two drawings. Then try a version using watercolour pencils or paint. See if you can use Cézanne's technique of making the fruits look 3-dimensional by only using patches of colour.

- Practise drawing using *one-point perspective*. You will need to fix a vanishing point which will be at eye-level and then all your horizontal lines should be angled towards that point. Then look again at Cézanne's painting and compare how the space is constructed inside your room and his.

- Paint a still life group in a room so you can see the front view and the top view of an object in the same picture.

methodical – a way of working through a process in regular, ordered steps.

one-point perspective – a system of perspective in which all the horizontal lines in a picture meet at one point. This point is at the eye level of the viewer and is called the vanishing point.

Content

The table in the front of this painting is covered with objects. A white tablecloth is draped over part of it, and pots and fruits are placed on top of it. In the back right hand corner of the table there is a large basket of fruit. Cézanne shows us objects from different angles at the same time so we look straight ahead at the front of the basket but then down onto the fruits inside it.

In earlier still life pictures like **Still Life with Ginger Jar, Sugar Bowl and Apples**, 1893–1894, Cézanne did not include details in the background. He wanted to concentrate his attention on the objects on the table so he painted in a simple background of coloured panels. **Still Life with Basket** is more ambitious and Cézanne has added details of furniture in the room.

Form

Cézanne did not draw this room using strict *perspective* but tried to show how he actually experienced being in the room. Our viewpoint changes as we scan the picture so we look straight forwards at the table, down at the fruits and then across the room to the chair in the far corner.

The objects on the table, as well as the table itself, are drawn from different viewpoints. The front edge of the table appears to break at the point where it is hidden by the cloth. On the left-hand side, we look down on top of the table but, on the right, we look straight on. The same happens with the large pot so it appears tipped up and we can almost see inside it. Cézanne believed this way of showing objects described more honestly the way we experience them.

Instead of *perspective* drawing Cézanne used colour to create a sense of depth. The far wall at the back of the picture is painted in dark reddy brown colours which go back in space. The orange colour of the table in the foreground and the bright red and apple greens of the fruits make this part of the painting come further forward.

Process

Cézanne wanted to show things were 3-dimensional in his paintings by only using colour. He did not want to draw outlines or use shading techniques to show the shape and form of objects. He thought these methods were 'illusionist tricks' used in academic painting and not really true to our experience of things. He wanted to paint objects just as he saw them and this was simply as a collection of various tones of colour.

The fruits are built up with patches of colour. The large round apple on the top of the basket has a yellowy green area which describes the part of the fruit which is nearest to us. Next to this is the red area which runs along the outside edge. By putting the *complementary colours* red and green next to each other Cézanne makes the fruit look rounded and 3-dimensional.

Cézanne creates an overall *harmony* of colours by balancing *complementary colours* throughout the painting. The blue of the pot, the piece of furniture on the left and the back wall balances out against the orange areas of the table and basket. Patches of red and green also balance out against each other.

Cézanne's brushstrokes build up layers of colour in patches. These dabs of colour form a pattern of coloured areas across the surface of the canvas.

Mood

There is a clear sense of order and structure in this painting. Even though Cézanne rejected the *traditional* methods of *perspective* and shading, the objects look solid and exist in a definite space in relation to each other.

Cézanne's painting has a direct impact which makes you feel you can share in his experience of the world. He has created a *harmonious composition* and at the same time tried to show truthfully the way we see and understand the things around us.

Mont Sainte-Victoire, 1904–1906, by Paul Cézanne

Kunstmuseum Basel

Background

The Mountain Sainte-Victoire was a landmark in the region of Aix-en-Provence where Cézanne lived. It was white limestone and about 1,000 metres high. Towards the end of his life, Cézanne painted it many times.

Cézanne started painting the mountain in the 1880s and normally chose a view with the mountain in the distance and a broad plain in front of it with trees and houses in it. In his first attempts to paint the scene, Cézanne kept quite closely to the *traditional* way of creating a sense of distance by using blue tones for the mountain in the background and warmer colours in the foreground (**Mont Sainte-Victoire**, 1885–1887).

However, Cézanne was not happy with this. He thought he was using an *artificial* method to create a sense of distance which was linked to *perspective* drawing. He wanted to paint a picture which was nearer to his own *perception* of landscape and free himself from the rules which had been handed down over hundreds of years.

Towards the end of his life his paintings of the mountain became more and more abstract. They have fascinated many artists including **Pablo Picasso** and **Henri Matisse** who said he was one of the most important and powerful influences on their work.

Ideas

- Make a print or tapestry (if you are doing textile design) from all, or a section, of Cézanne's painting of the Mountain Sainte-Victoire. Pick out the main blocks of colour and try to match the tones.

- The Impressionist, Auguste Renoir, painted the same view of the mountain (**Mont Sainte-Victoire**, 1889). He has tried to capture the effect of sunlight and has used warm colours in the foreground and cool violet tones in the background to create the effect of distance. Compare the different styles of Cézanne's picture with Renoir's. Try to make a study of the two.

- Make your own series of paintings from a landscape of your choice. Try to analyse the shapes in the landscape like Cézanne has. Develop your paintings into abstract colour compositions.

Mont Sainte-Victoire (1889) by Pierre Auguste Renoir
The Barnes Foundation, Merion, Pennsylvania, USA

Content

In the 1880s Cézanne painted several views of the mountain from a distance at his sister's farm, south-west of where he lived in Aix-en-Provence. When he returned to it in the early 1900s he had a much closer view from his new studio at Les Lauves.

Cézanne gives the huge cone-shaped mountain a far more dominant place in these later pictures. The fields and little village spread out in a broad plane beneath it and there are patches of dark green woodland.

Form

Cézanne did not want to just reproduce a scene from nature but wanted to make a picture which was a *harmonious* design by itself. In fact he said that what he was aiming at in his landscapes was to paint '*a harmony in parallel with nature*'.

He did not aim at a traditional *perspective* view of the mountain in the landscape. He tried to get closer to his true *perception* of the scene in front of him by building up a tight arrangement of colours.

The patches of colour form a loose grid or pattern across the surface of the painting. On the left-hand side, the shapes of the trees are continued with patches of green paint into the sky. This merges the foreground into the background and increases the effect of an overall pattern.

Cezanne brings his painting to the edge of *abstract art* but never totally gives up the subject of his paintings. In fact he worked directly from the landscape most of his life and, although he makes us very aware of his brushstrokes and pattern, we can still see the mountain and surrounding landscape quite clearly.

Process

With directional brushstrokes Cézanne describes the different planes in the landscape. Sometimes he smears the paint on thickly with a palette knife as if he is making a sculpture on the canvas.

Cézanne creates a *luminous* yellow area where the houses are in the middle of the picture. This is like a band of light leading to the mountain. By contrast, the shadowy areas of woodland are made up of dark violet and green tones.

The mountain is painted mainly in cool blue colours but patches of blue are then repeated throughout the painting creating a unity of pattern and colour. Cézanne often used this striking blue colour in all of his paintings of the mountain and said, 'One must add enough blue to make the air *tactile*'.

Mood

This painting makes us think about the way we actually see things and make sense of the world around us. Cézanne has constructed an intricate, patterned surface which at the same time is an accurate description of where things are in the landscape he is painting.

Cézanne has found a new way of understanding how and what we see without using the *conventional* means of *perspective* drawing and tone to show distance. He has constructed a beautiful painting, which has its own internal structure, by building up layers of *harmonious* colours.

Glossary

abstract art – art which calls attention to shape, colour and form rather than making an object or landscape look recognisable.

allegory – a story which refers to literature or myth which has a deeper meaning.

anarchist – a political group who believed that people should be able to organise themselves without having governments.

anonymous – nameless and unknown.

applied arts – areas of design where artists' skills are used to produce things for a set purpose like posters and furniture.

arbitrary – based on opinion not research.

art establishment – those people who are recognised as being the authority on art. They included the Royal Academicians and the Salon jury who thought that art should only show idealised scenes of people and places.

artefact – a product of human art and workmanship such as a clay pot, poster, furniture, etc.

artificial – man made not natural.

avant garde – a military term given to the art movement which was the most recent, shocking and ground breaking.

Buddhist – a follower of the Eastern religion called Buddhism in which people believed in the enlightened one, or Buddha.

caricatures – a way of sketching a person which is over-done and often grotesque.

catalogue – a book which lists artworks displayed in an exhibition and also has essays in it which describe and explain the work.

classical – following the rules of art first set out in ancient Greece and Rome.

classical proportion – the ancient Greeks worked out a system of proportion or balance which was based on what they thought was the ideal human body. When used in painting it means things are evenly spaced across the picture which gives a feeling of balance.

Cloissonism – a style of painting developed by Paul Gauguin which was based on medieval stained glass windows and enamels. He painted thick black lines around areas of bright colour.

colonialist and colonies – when the government of one country takes over and settles in other lands. Tahiti was a French colony.

Communism, Communist – someone who believes that the community should share all work and property according to wants and needs.

composition – the layout or formal design of a picture.

complementary colours – colours which are opposite each other in the colour wheel, for example, blue and orange, purple and yellow, green and red.

Constructivism – an artistic movement in Russia where artists like Vladimir Tatlin and Naum Gabo wanted to 'construct' a new kind of art using abstract shapes and forms.

conventional – following traditional or accepted rules.

conte – compressed charcoal.

contemplation, contemplate – to look or think about something, to meditate on it.

contours – the outline or shape of something.

critic – someone who judges art and writes their opinions for the public.

Cubism – Cubist – a style of painting developed in 1908 by Georges Braque and Pablo Picasso. They made paintings which showed things from different angles at the same time and broke up their pictures into geometric shapes like cubes and triangles.

depression – a state of mind which brings about deep sadness / melancholy.

distort – to twist or stretch something in to a different shape, to deform it.

Divisionism – Divisionist – a style of painting developed by Georges Seurat and Paul Signac in which colours are split up into dots and dashes of primary colour. When you stand back from the painting you mix the colours visually. In their later work they used only dots of paint and this was called Pointillism.

durable – lasting.

dynamic – forceful, exciting, energetic and full of movement.

enamelling – a method of decorating metal which results in a brightly coloured, glass-like surface.

enigmatic – mysterious, hard to understand.

exotic – things from foreign countries which are strikingly different.

Expressionism – Expressionist – a group of artists who believed that the most important thing was them to express their own thoughts and feelings rather than follow traditional rules of art.

fanatic – someone who becomes over enthusiastic and obsessed with a cause.

Fauves – comes from a French word meaning 'wild beasts'. In 1905, this name was given to a group of artists led by Henri Matisse who painted using a bold and shocking style with very bright colours.

frieze – horizontal broad band of sculpture at the top of a Greek temple or other work of art.

Futurism – Futurists – the Futurists were a group of Italian artists, such as Giacomo Balla and Umberto Boccioni, who were working around 1909. They loved big cities, speed and machinery and tried to show movement in their paintings by using the painting styles of Divisionism and Cubism.

grotesque – something that is horribly distorted and often frightening.

harmony / harmonious – being in agreement and peaceful.

impasto – to build paint up on the canvas in very thick layers.

Impressionism – Impressionist – Impressionism was an art movement in France between 1860 and 1880. Artists used new painting methods to create scenes from modern life.

intensity – a depth or strength of feeling which is almost too much to take.

luminous – glowing with light.

materialistic – when you value money or possessions more than anything else.

medieval – belonging to the Middle Ages which started around the 11th century and finished in the 15th century.

meditation – a peaceful state of mind in which the person is in deep thought.

melancholy – a state of deep sadness and depression.

methodical – a way of working through a process in regular, ordered steps.

monumental – an art object that is usually massive, permanent and imposing.

Nabis – a group of Symbolist artists which included Paul Serusier, Edouard Vuillard and Pierre Bonnard. They took the name 'Nabis' from the Hebrew word meaning 'prophet' and followed the work of Paul Gauguin.

Neo-Impressionism – Seurat's style of painting was called by several names – Neo-Impressionism, Divisionism and Pointillism. It was called Neo-Impressionism because Seurat built on the colour work of the Impressionists but analysed colour in a very scientific way.

one-point perspective – a system of perspective in which all the horizontal lines in a picture meet at one point. This point is at the eye level of the viewer and is called the vanishing point.

optically – visually, relating to the eye and how we see.

optimism – a hopeful way of looking at the world in which you expect good things to happen.

perception / perceive – the way we understand the world through our senses such as seeing and touching and our thought processes..

perspective – a way of constructing a picture from a particular viewpoint as though you were looking through a window into it.

Pointillism – Pointillist – In Seurat's later work he covered his paintings with tiny points or dots of paint. When you stood back from his pictures the colours glowed with light.

primitive – term given by Europeans to ancient societies in countries like Africa and South America. They thought these societies lived closer to nature and still had ancient customs and tribal rituals.

radiate – to shine out in all directions.

rituals – religious rites, acts or customs done over and over again.

Salon – annual exhibition of the French Royal Academy of Painting and Sculpture.

Salon d'Automne – an exhibition held in the autumn.

Salon des Indépendants – exhibitions started in 1884 by Seurat and Signac in opposition to the official Salon.

Salon des Refusés – exhibition of paintings refused by the Salon.

simultaneous contrast – a way of shading developed by Georges Seurat in which dark areas of tone are put next to light areas. This creates a contrast in which the edge of the dark area looks darker and the light edge looks lighter.

social-realist – a realistic style of art which claimed to show the true situation of people in society.

spiritual – involving the inner, unworldly side of human understanding.

symbol and *symbolic* – a sign or object which stands in for, and refers to, a hidden or deeper meaning.

Symbolists – the Symbolist movement involved writers as well as artists. Symbolists were against realism in art and wanted to create pictures which were more imaginative and dreamlike.

Symbolist manifesto – a written statement of the aims and ideas of Symbolism.

Synthetic Symbolists – there were two groups of Symbolist artists– literary symbolists painted pictures which referred to mythical or mysterious events and synthetic symbolists linked their work to music and painted with strong, bright colours.

symmetrical – balanced, the same on both sides.

tactile – able to be touched and felt.

traditional – a tried and tested way of doing things which is often handed down from one generation to another.

tranquility – calm, peacefulness.

transient – short-lived, passing opposite to lasting.

unrealistic – something that does not look like a recognisable object or landscape.

urban – living or situated in a city or town.

vibrant – vivid, thrilling.

wet-in-wet – a painting technique in which the artist does not allow the first layer of paint to dry before adding more paint, usually in a different colour on top.

Timeline

1839 Paul Cézanne born on 19th January

1848 Paul Gauguin born on 7th June

1853 Vincent Van Gogh born on 30th March

1859 Georges Seurat born 2nd December

1863 Paul Signac born 11th November

1863 Exhibition at Salon des Refusés (showed many works that had been rejected by the Salon jury including Manet's **Déjeuner sur l'Herbe**)

1864 Paul Serusier born 9th November

1867 Pierre Bonnard born on 3rd October

1868 Edouard Vuillard born 11th November

1870 Maurice Denis born on 25th November

1870 Beginning of Franco-Prussian War

1874 First Impressionist Exhibition

1877 Raoul Dufy born on 3rd June

1880 Andre Derain born on 17th June

1882 Seventh Impressionist Exhibition

1883 Collapse of the French economy and Gauguin loses his job on the stockmarket and begins to paint full-time

1884 Establishment of the Salon des Indépendants

1886 Van Gogh goes to Paris and sees Impressionist work for the first time

1886 Eighth and last Impressionist Exhibition – Seurat exhibits **A Sunday Afternoon on the Island of La Grande Jatte**; Gauguin exhibits 19 paintings from his first trip to Brittany

1886 Seurat exhibits seven paintings with the new Les Vingt group of artists in Belgium

1886 Emile Zola publishes his novel *L'Oeuvre* (The Work) based on Cézanne which causes a rift between the two friends

1888 Van Gogh leaves Paris in May and goes to Arles in the South of France

1888 Gauguin completes **Vision after the Sermon**

1888 The foundation of the Nabis

1888 October, Gauguin joins Van Gogh in Arles in south France

1889 January, Van Gogh goes into the Saint Paul Asylum in Saint-Remy for treatment

1889 May, Van Gogh discharges himself from hospital and goes to small village outside Paris called Auvers-sur-Oise where he receives therapy from Dr Gachet

1889 Universal Exhibition takes place in Paris

1889 Gauguin exhibits **Vision after the Sermon** in an exhibition called 'The Impressionist and Synthetist Group' at the Café Volpini in the Universal Exhibition. He becomes the leader of the Synthetist Symbolist group and the Nabis

1889 Cézanne, Van Gogh and Gauguin exhibit with the Les Vingt group of artists in Belgium

1890 27th July, Van Gogh attempts suicide by shooting himself and dies 2 days later on the 29th July

1891 April, Gauguin leaves for first trip to Tahiti

1891 Seurat has another successful exhibition with the Belgian group called Les Vingt

1891 16th March, Seurat exhibited his painting called **The Circus** at the Salon des Independants

1891 29th March, Seurat dies from a sudden illness

1893 Gauguin returns to France

1894 December, Gauguin leaves France for good and returns to Tahiti

1895 Ambroise Vollard, well-known art dealer, organises exhibition of Cézanne 's work

1898 Solo exhibition of Cézanne 's work

1899 Solo exhibition of Cézanne 's work

1903 Gauguin dies on 8th May

1904	Exhibition of independent artists at the Salon d'Automne
1906	Cézanne dies on 22nd October
1910	Manet and the Post-Impressionists exhibition organised by Roger Fry in London
1912	Second Post-Impressionist exhibition organised by Roger Fry in London
1914	Beginning of World War 1

Resource List

Books for further reading

Europe Transformed 1878–1919 by Norman Stone, Fontana, 1983

Post-Impressionism by Ian Barras Hill, Galley Press, 1980

Post-Impressionism by Belinda Thomson, Cambridge University Press, 1998

Post-Impressionism by Bernard Denvir, Thames and Hudson, 1992

Post-Impressionism from Van Gogh to Gauguin by J. Rewald, Secker and Warburg, 1978

Symbolist Art by Edward Lucie-Smith, Thames and Hudson, 1972

The Post-Impressionists by Martha Kapos, Hugh Lauter Levin Associates, 1993

Bonnard: Colour and Light by Nicholas Watkins, Tate Gallery Publishing, 1998

Cézanne by Nicola Nonhoff, Konemann, 1999

Cézanne by Marcel Brion, Thames and Hudson, 1974

Cézanne by Catherine Dean, Phaidon Press, 1994

Gauguin by Robert Anderson, Franklin Watts, 2003

Gauguin – The Primitive Sophisticate by Ingo F. Walther, Taschen, 2000

Gauguin by Belinda Thomson, Thames and Hudson, 1987

Gauguin by Linda Bolton, Tiger Books, 1997

Gauguin and the School of Pont-Aven by W. Jaworska, Thames and Hudson, 1972

Van Gogh by Ingo F. Walther, Taschen, 2000

Van Gogh by Andrew Forrest, Hodder and Stoughton, 2002

Van Gogh, Gauguin and the Impressionist Circle by M. Roskill Thames and Hudson, 1970

Vincent Van Gogh: The Painter and the Portrait by George T. M. Shackelford, Universe Publishing, 2000

Seurat – The Master of Pointillism by Hajo Duchting, Taschen, 1999

Seurat by Sarah Carr-Gomm, Studio Editions Ltd., 1993

Seurat by J. Russell, Thames and Hudson, 1976

Seurat by R. Thomson, Phaidon, 1985

Paul Signac by Marina Ferretti Bocquillon et al, Harry N. Abrams, Inc., 2000

Vuillard by Guy Cogeval, Thames and Hudson, 2002

Vuillard, Royal Academy of Arts, London, Exhibition Catalogue, co-published by Guy **Cogeval**, The Montreal Museum of Fine Arts and the National Gallery of Art, Washington, 2004

Useful web sites

www.artchive.com

www.artnet.com

www.courtauld.ac.uk

www.musee-orsay.fr

www.nationalgallery.org.uk

www.vangoghmuseum.nl

www.moma.org

Photographic Credits

If you enjoyed this book why not read ...

A Flying StART: Impressionism
A Flying StART: Expressionism
A Flying StART: Surrealism

By Pam Cutler

A series of illustrated art reference books designed for children with dyslexia and other reading difficulties. Clarity of language and layout ensures these readers can access and appreciate art. Written by Pam Cutler from the Moat School, an expert in the fields of art and dyslexia.

- Critical analysis of the artists' work explained
- Tips on how to research and evaluate an artist's work
- Enables students studying GCSE, standard grades and highers to complete specific research for their exams

Impressionism
ISBN 1-842991-76-0

Expressionism
ISBN 1-842991-77-9

Surrealism
ISBN 1-842991-80-9

You can order these books direct from:

Macmillan Distribution Ltd, Brunel Road, Houndmills, Basingstoke, Hampshire RG21 6XS

Tel 01256 302699

Email mdl@macmillan.co.uk